Štěpánka Sekaninová
Linh Dao

WELCOME TO THE ANTHILL

albatros

ON THE EDGE OF THE FOREST

Oh look, what's that big mound on the edge of the forest?! It's absolutely teeming with life! Let's take a closer look. We need to be very quiet, though, so we don't disturb anyone. Do you know what it is? It's a perfectly constructed anthill full of ants. What do you say? Shall we pay them a visit?

SPRING

Hey there! Over here! At the top of the anthill! If you think I'm just lounging around sunbathing, you're wrong. I'm absorbing the heat of the sun's rays, so I can help heat up the anthill with my body. Now that I'm nice and toasty, let's go explore the inside of the ant colony.

Here in the anthill, we're not big fans of the cold. So we keep the temperature between 77 and 86 degrees Fahrenheit. In wintertime, to stop the heat from escaping, we close the ventilation holes by simply sealing them with the same material used to build the anthill . . . like we're doing right now. And when it gets too hot for us in the summer, we just remove the seal to let in fresh air.

A PASSAGE THROUGH THE ANTHILL

Our anthill is a really ingenious structure. On the surface you see a six-foot-tall mound covered with a layer of pine needles, but below the ground it runs much deeper. It's a tangled network of passageways and chambers fortified with twigs. Anyone who doesn't live here will never find their way around it and will soon get lost.

We'll take a right here, then a left, then turn right again, and here we are in the chamber where we keep our food supplies for the winter. The winters can be long and harsh, so we have to make sure that we have what we need to make it through.

HOW WE WORK

There are loads of workers in our ant colony – so many that you wouldn't be able to count us. We're just one big family... and a very hardworking family at that. Every member of the colony has a special task, which is very important for our survival.

GUARDS

Guards stand like soldiers at the entrances to the anthill and guard them vigilantly against intruders. They won't allow anyone to endanger our home.

CLEANERS

Cleaners make sure everything is in its right place, so that the anthill is clean, tidy, and cozy.

REPAIRERS

Whenever anything in the anthill is damaged or broken, nest maintenance workers will immediately get to work fixing it. They don't want to be blamed for the anthill falling on everyone's heads. They also make sure that we keep the right temperature inside our home.

BUILDERS

Builders are workers who construct the anthill, expand it, and build new chambers and corridors. They start out as babysitters and later become builders.

BABYSITTERS

Babysitters are the ones who patiently raise each new generation of ants. They protect the eggs, feed the larvae, and look after the pupas. Babysitters tend to be young workers, and this is their first job in the anthill.

FORAGERS

Foragers are strong and super fit. They spend the whole day outside running around gathering materials to build and repair the anthill. They collect sticks, twigs, pine needles, and resin from trees. Resin is very important for ants . . . you'll soon see why.

HUNTERS

Skilled and seasoned female hunters supply our ant family with food. Every day, no matter the weather, they venture out into the world to hunt prey and seek out good things to eat. Sometimes they bring us live and dead insects, and sometimes berries full of sweet juice.

TENDERS

The tenders job is to raise aphids. These female ants care for and protect them from anything that might want to eat them, such as ladybugs. In return, the aphids provide the ants with delicious honeydew. Look at how it's done. This tender is milking an aphid for its sweet juice.

BOY ANTS

Boy ants don't have to do any work. They just lounge around the anthill waiting for their big day – the day of their wedding flight. Their one and only task, which is extremely important, is to mate with the young queens.

ANTHILL CLEANING

Watch out! There's a big anthill cleanup in progress right now. Over there, the maintenance ants are plugging a hole made by a deer's hoof... once again the cleaners are spreading resin. Remember how I said resin is important? It's because resin protects our anthills from mold and bacteria. We also spray ant acid over everything, because it's very effective for cleaning.

WHAT'S THAT BIRD DOING?

Unfortunately, some woodland birds enjoy rolling around in anthills, and they end up demolishing our homes. It's not that they mean us harm – they just want to get rid of all the parasites in their feathers. A shower of acid is the perfect way to ask them to please leave.

A STABLE FOR APHIDS

The weather outside must be getting worse. The tenders are plucking the aphids from the stems of plants and bringing them into the comfort of the stables inside our anthill. It's true that our aphids are normally kept outside in the pasture, where they feed on plant stems or branches, but during the winter and in poor weather, they are carried carefully inside. Over the winter, we take good care of the aphid eggs. That way, we always have a large flock.

MILKING APHIDS

Look at all that lovely honeydew! A tender is milking an aphid for its sweet juice. It's easy to do! She just tickles its underbelly with her antennae and the jug fills right up. After that, the tender washes the aphid with a drop of dew to keep it clean. And can you guess why our aphids are so beautifully plump? It's because the tenders move them from plant to plant as they eat to their heart's content. This way, they're never hungry and can make lots of sweet honeydew for us.

AN AUDIENCE WITH THE QUEEN

Welcome to our queen's abode. Please show her due respect. She is much larger than us common ants and also lives much longer. While we workers live for five years, the queen can live up to twenty – that's more than any other insect! Her main role is to lay eggs, and she lays and lays them all day long.

In early spring, the queen lays eggs from which will hatch new queens and winged boy ants. In summer and autumn, she then lays eggs that will become our future workers. It's very hard work. She will lay over 100 million eggs in her lifetime! To make the queen's life easier, we are here to provide for all her needs. We feed her, clean her, and tell her what's going on outside.

ANT NURSERY

Shhh! We have to be really quiet now. We're entering the closely guarded ward for newborn and baby ants. This is where the eggs laid by our queen are brought by the cleaner ants and placed neatly side by side, sticking them together. The babysitter ants have to lick the eggs to keep them moist and to clean off all the bacteria.

LOOK, LARVAE!

Oh look – here come the hungry larvae! The babysitters are cleaning them and feeding them food from their stomachs. That way, they grow nicely. When the nursery is no longer comfortable, they are immediately moved to a room where the temperature and humidity is perfect for their further development. Oh look, there's Laura the babysitter with a bunch of larvae!

HATCHING PUPAS
This is the chamber of pupas. It's a kind of ant maternity ward. Take a look – a new ant is coming into the world. It's a good thing too, as there's a ton of work to do and everyone's help is needed. Even so, every newborn ant has to wait until its body has hardened before it can work.
14 days
10 more days
14 more days
an egg
a larva
a pupa
DEVELOPMENT FROM EGG TO ADULT ANT
an adult ant

ROYAL BABIES

All the eggs, larvae, and pupas here are clearly much, much larger than those in the other chambers. Since this is where the new queens and young winged boy ants will develop and hatch, the larvae here receive different food than the larvae of ordinary worker ants. The babysitters feed them a special, highly nutritious ant milk.

Everything must be spotless for the royal babies.
Z Z Z

THE NEW QUEEN AND THE WEDDING FLIGHT

Oh, what a lovely day! We're about to witness an extraordinary event. The new queens have hatched, and so have the boy ants. The whole anthill is getting ready for their wedding flight! We're decorating the halls and preparing a banquet. We're singing and rejoicing, and looking forward to the day when they'll leave home.

THIS IS HOW IT GOES

All the winged queens, along with their suitors, fly away from the anthill to perform their wedding dances in the air. It's called swarming. Once the young ant lords have mated with their noble queens, they go out into the world and try to start new anthills or take over those of other ants. It's no easy task, and they don't always emerge victorious. But when they do, the new queen sheds her wings in her new home, secludes herself in her royal chamber, and starts laying eggs.

ANT TALK

Want to know how we ants communicate? We greet with our antennae, share scents to show hunger, and use smells to express everything from friendship to danger. Our scents help us recognize each other, care for eggs, signal the queen, and warn of threats. When an ant dies, its scent lets us know it's time for a funeral. Every smell tells a story!

I'M HUNGRY

If one ant has an empty belly and another has just eaten a bunch, the full ant will gladly share her food with her hungry friend. She wouldn't want a friend with a rumbling tummy.

I'D KNOW THAT SMELL ANYWHERE.

Another way we ants communicate is through our scent. All ants from the same anthill smell like our home, and we could recognize each other even if we were on the other side of the world.

BEWARE, ENEMY!

Yikes, an enemy is approaching! As soon as we know that we are under threat from an uninvited intruder, we sound the alarm. How, you ask? With our scent! The strength of the scent depends on how dangerous the threat is.

A NOBLE ODOR

Of course, the queen smells of royalty . . . Her scent makes the ants in her royal retinue serve her with ultimate devotion until their last breath.

BABY SCENT

Even unborn ants have a scent. Our babysitter ants can tell our eggs apart from those of other ants by how they smell. And they can also tell how old baby ants are by their scent.

LAST WHIFF

When an ant dies, its scent changes, so the cleaners in charge of the ant's funeral know immediately that their friend has passed away.

ANT GUESTS INVITED AND UNINVITED

UNINVITED GUEST

Oh no, look! That beetle lurking on the edge of our anthill has a sinister plan. It often stands there watching us, waiting to pounce on a lone ant that can't defend itself.

But we won't let it! If it makes one move, we'll swarm all over it and give it a thrashing! Beetles aren't the only ones with fearsome jaws.

GUESTS WE HARDLY NOTICE

We also have harmless guests in our anthill. They roam our corridors feeding on any leftovers they can find. The remains of pupas, egg shells, and leftover food – that sort of thing. As long as they don't try to eat our babies, it's just fine. We have a harmonious relationship with these little bugs.

DOMESTICATED GUESTS

We also have *invited* guests . . . Come and take a look. They're beetles we've hatched from tiny larvae. We keep them in our chambers and feed and protect them, but they're not allowed to leave our anthill. They can't take a single step outside. Of course, we are fond of these guests, because their secretions liven up our diet . . .

BRRR, IT'S GETTING CHILLY ...

That means winter is approaching. Soon, we'll have to start preparing. We'll need to seal all the entrances and any other holes in our anthill. Once this is done, we'll descend to the deepest chambers at the very bottom of the anthill. There, we'll have a nice long sleep until springtime.

. . . zzz
zzz . . .

A NEW HOUSE

What's happening over there at the edge of the woods? There's a whole lot of building activity going on! It looks like a new anthill is going up. Ants are scurrying around all over the place. Some are searching for materials, others are using them to build their new home. There's a lot of backbreaking work ahead, so let's leave these industrious creatures to get on with their task. So long, little ants!

Look, we're going to have new neighbors! Hope you'll come back and visit us again.

WELCOME TO THE ANTHILL

Written by Štěpánka Sekaninová
Illustrated by Linh Dao

5. května 1746/22, Prague 4, Czech Republic
Author: Štěpánka Sekaninová

Translator: Mark Worthington
Editor: Scott Alexander Jones

Printed in China by Leo Paper Group Ltd.

www.albatrosbooks.com